Senturion

A Predictive Political Simulation Model

Mark Abdollahian, Michael Baranick, Brian Efird, and Jacek Kugler

Center for Technology and National Security Policy
National Defense University

July 2006

Mark Abdollahian, Ph.D. is a Research Professor at the School of Politics and Economics at Claremont Graduate University and Chief Operating Officer at Sentia Group, Inc.. Dr. Abdollahian can be contacted at MAA@sentiagroup.com.

Michael Baranick, Ph.D. is a Senior Research Fellow at the Center for Technology and National Security Policy, National Defense University. Dr. Baranick can be contacted at BaranickM@ndu.edu.

Brian Efird, Ph.D. is an Executive Vice President at Sentia Group, Inc.. Dr. Efird can be contacted at BAE@sentiagroup.com.

Jacek Kugler, Ph.D. is the Elisabeth Helm Rosecrans Professor of International Relations and Political Economy in the Department of Politics and Policy, School of Politics and Economics at Claremont Graduate University. Dr. Kugler can be contacted at jacek.kugler@cgu.edu.

Defense & Technology Papers are published by the National Defense University Center for Technology and National Security Policy, Fort Lesley J. McNair, Washington, DC. CTNSP publications are available online at http://www.ndu.edu/ctnsp/publications.html.

Contents

Introduction

The expanding complexity of sub-national and cross-national threats to national security strains the analytical capabilities of the Department of Defense (DOD) and the Intelligence Community, highlighting the need for methods and tools that can make this emergent complexity manageable. With an ever-increasing spectrum of threats, more objective analytic capabilities that draw on all-source intelligence and advances in computational methods are needed to help provide insight and aid understanding of individual and group behavior.

Computer-based predictive technologies have the maturity, track record, and capability to help meet this challenge. Just as DOD and the Intelligence Community apply computational modeling for knowledge discovery applications, so too can computational technologies be applied to improve the understanding of human behavior and decisionmaking. Moreover, the approach described in this paper relies not on the large volume of electronic data focused on by most computational methods, but rather provides a platform to facilitate and pool the knowledge of subject matter experts in the Federal Government and academia. Computational modeling based on reliable simulations of human behavior can then be applied to this information set to form the basis for unbiased predictions of potential threats. This combination of technologies can then form the basis for courses of action in response to a more systematic assessment of potential threats.

This paper summarizes work utilizing the Senturion predictive analysis software at the National Defense University (NDU). The Center for Technology and National Security Policy (CTNSP) at NDU has been testing the Senturion capability since 2002, and has begun to support the application of this new technology in DOD. In this paper, we begin by describing the methodology underlying the software, and then provide an overview of three case studies that used the software: a predictive analysis of the stabilization and reconstruction phase of Operation *Iraqi Freedom* (OIF), the run-up to the Iraqi elections in January 2005, and the leadership transition in Palestine following the death of Yasser Arafat.

Each of these projects tested the application of the software's modeling technology to unfolding events. Each analysis was performed and briefed to senior government decisionmakers well in advance of events; the forecasts from each project tracked well with reality, often providing counterintuitive results. The approach provides policymakers and analysts with a tool for anticipating the outcome of complex political events that can also provide a detailed explanation of why events may not unfold as expected with traditional means of analysis.

Senturion is a simulation capability that analyzes the political dynamics within local, domestic, and international contexts and predicts how the policy positions of competing interests will evolve over time. The underlying methodology relies on agent-based modeling—an approach that applies a set of mathematical algorithms against rules that structure a simulation of the behavior of "agents," which in this case are the individuals and groups that influence political outcomes. The set of rules used by Senturion synthesize several classes of political science and microeconomic theories into a real-world decisionmaking tool for researchers and practitioners. Rather than a statistical or probabilistic approach to predictive modeling, Senturion employs a set of algorithms drawn from game theory, decision theory, spatial bargaining, and microeconomics.

Each theory provides a functional component for modeling how agents interact in a political process. The Senturion methodology has been applied across diverse fields, including diplomacy, military campaigns, economic accords and business negotiations. The simulation software yields unique risk-mitigation benefits by anticipating and explaining outcomes and identifying courses of action to achieve beneficial change.

Senturion helps analysts frame key political issues that either propel or impede policy objectives. Given a particular issue, the software facilitates subject matter expert identification of the positions of critical stakeholders on policy issues, weighs their potential influence, and assesses the strength of their commitment or advocacy of a policy position. This subject matter expert-generated data input captures a *snapshot* of the current political landscape with a high degree of accuracy. However, the track record of analysts' predictions is typically accurate 45 to 65 percent of the time.[1] The agent-based modeling approach allows for a consistent, systematic, significantly less-biased, and accurate analysis of the evolution of political dynamics given the subject matter expert-generated political landscape. Halal and Bojes (2005) conducted a survey of experts in the field of forecasting to determine which methodologies are more useful and accurate in applied forecasting. Among the algorithms Senturion relies on as rules for the behavior of its agents, the survey identified many to be valuable forecasting methodologies. In particular, the combination of expert interviews, simulation, and game theory draws upon some of the highest-evaluated approaches to predictive analysis. Precursors to the Senturion approach focused more on the calculation of coalitional support for different policy alternatives, as opposed to a dynamic model that simulates the interaction of individuals and groups over time.[2]

Stakeholder Analyses

Politics has often been called the "art of the possible." If economics is the study of the distribution of scarce resources, then politics is the competition for the rules that govern the distribution of those scarce resources. Ultimately, these possibilities are created and constrained by individual, groups, nation-states and their interactions. In the 1960s, work in the field of business and management on understanding how individuals influence outcomes led to stakeholder analyses.[3] Political issues at the policy level might encompass U.S. policy in a particular country or region, budgetary allocations in Congress, national autonomy, wars of liberation, troop deployments, or even pipeline placement—any question that is fundamentally determined by the interaction of people.

Traditional stakeholder analysis has relied on qualitative assessments of stakeholder preferences as the basis for predictions of how stakeholders are likely to behave in forming coalitions in favor of or in opposition to political issues. Senturion relies on identifying primary, secondary, and tertiary stakeholders who have an interest in propelling or impeding various political outcomes. Once stakeholders are identified by subject matter experts, they are categorized by their ability to influence outcomes and the importance of political issues to them. This categorization characteristically translates into matrix mapping with four typologies:

---

[1] See Rieber (2004).

[2] For a review see Feder (1987) and Kugler and Feng (1997).

[3] *Stakeholder* refers to persons, institutions, agencies, private sector groups, governments, non-state actors, or other entities with a stake in the outcome, or more importantly, some potential to influence a particular outcome.

- Large influencers with high importance who can either help or impede progress. Opponents should be isolated, while proponents should be empowered to form larger coalitions.
- Large influencers with little importance who can be mobilized to assist the political process if they support it, or blocked if they oppose it.
- Small influencers with high importance who can either help or impede progress. Opponents should be isolated, while proponents should be empowered in stronger coalitions.
- Small influencers with little importance who could be motivated to assist the political process, if necessary, but would not be worth the effort to block.

Other methodologies attempt to aggregate specific stakeholder interests or scale their influence or importance. But these approaches lack a dynamic, analytical component that allows observers to know what will happen over time. This traditional stakeholder analysis may enlighten, but it does not answer the key operational question, "what's next?"

Work in the 1970s resulted in a more formal specification of the stakeholder approach, deriving the particular political issue as a linear continuum that stakeholders fight on with a consistent set of data inputs in the Prince System.[4] Thus, stakeholders were assigned particular influence, importance, and positional attributes that could be scaled to arrive at a relative ranking of political viability but not actual political outcomes. The reality of most political processes is that stakeholders exert influence to shape the dynamics of outcomes based on interactions with each other.[5] Tracking these dynamics and capturing the knowledge to achieve a desired outcome is a complex process. One approach suggests employing vectors in static form to anticipate stakeholder bargaining dynamics.[6] Such solutions are relatively straightforward in dyadic interactions but become less predictable in multiple-actor environments. Worse, analysts are forced to simplify and aggregate stakeholders into larger, coarser groups to reach any conclusions, often missing important details. This is further complicated when multiple political issues are present.[7] Combining traditional stakeholder analysis with recent advances in agent-based modeling allows for the accurate and rich simulation of all stakeholders on a particular political issue.

Methodology

Over the last thirty years, a large, multidisciplinary literature on the simulation of individual and group behavior on political issues has emerged and, more recently, proliferated.[8] Approaches in this field typically focus on agents at the micro level (individuals or small groups) as the unit of analysis. The simulation technology used by Senturion models the behavior and interaction of decisionmakers (such as individuals, families, and firms) within a larger system. This modeling

---

[4] For a review of the PRINCE System see Coplin and O'Leary (1972).

[5] For more detail see Bueno de Mesquita (1981) and (1985).

[6] For more detail an initial notion of applying vectors to stakeholder analysis see Lalman (1988).

[7] This notion is explored in more technical detail in Morrow (1986), Morgan (1994), and Abdollahian and Alsharabati (1995) and (2003).

[8] The literature here is rather broad. A sample can be found in Axtell, Axelrod, Epstein, and Cohen (1996); Epstein and Axtel (1996); Chwe (1999); and Axlerod and Tesfatsion (2005).

strategy uses data on representative samples of decisionmakers, along with equations and algorithms representing behavioral processes, to simulate the evolution through time of each decisionmaker, hence, of the entire population of decisionmakers.[9]

Whereas the computational capacity of thirty years ago allowed the simulation of only very limited numbers of agents, or stakeholders, today's computational power allows for sophisticated rule sets to be applied to thousands of agents simultaneously. The stakeholder model embedded in Senturion—which is technically an agent-based model, because agents are interacting within a system of rules—transcends traditional stakeholder approaches by providing a consistent and systematic modeled framework for the exponentially increasing network of interactions without reduction or simplification in problem fidelity. For a given political issue, Senturion simulates the iterative political decisionmaking calculus among stakeholders with different interests in and varying influence on the political process. With considerable accuracy, it can predict how these bargaining dynamics play out across a network of political relations over time. The result is an analytical assessment of the likely extent of reform and of the degree of stakeholder support for this outcome *a priori* without reliance on an *ad hoc* assessment.

Beginning with a rigorous subject matter expert-led data collection process, one can obtain a detailed depiction of the current political landscape. In the data-collection process, stakeholders are assigned multiple attributes of their political position and potential influence. This is followed by an assessment of the amount of political, economic, social, and military capital they are willing to expend on the issue. Thus, all agents are not created equal *de novo*. They possess unique and individual capabilities that help determine their interactions with other agents. All agents are subject to the same push and pull of the political process, trying to maximize their available resources to support or oppose a particular outcome. Senturion views all agents as attempting to maximize their interests and seeking to create coalitions to support those interests.

Senturion's rule- and equation-based algorithms model the intuition behind each stakeholder's political calculus by breaking the process into sub-elements that can be modeled. Each element models a particular part of the decision process; by combining the elements sequentially, the approach can provide an assessment and explanation of how stakeholders arrive at a particular decision or political outcome. Each sub-element of the modeling process is designed to help predict a part of how stakeholder positions will change and thus predict the evolution of the policy process in toto. From an analytical perspective, dynamic and recursive estimation of stakeholder interactions allows Senturion to anticipate compromises and coalitions that will form in response to political pressures. The end result is a simulation capability that provides both a forecast and a detailed explanation and justification for its predictions. (See figure 1 for a conceptual overview of Senturion's sub-element rules).

---

[9] See Caldwell (1997).

1. Initial Stakeholder Data

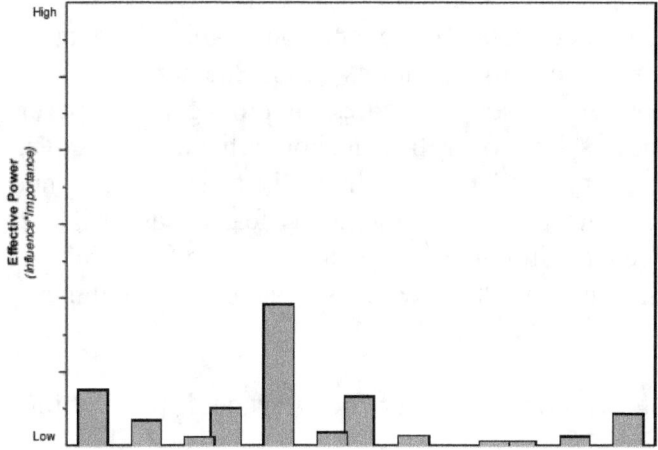

2. Agent Based Rules & Modeling Elements

1. What is winning coalition or Median position?

2. Given the winning coalition position, which groups are risk taking?

3. How does each stakeholder view every other stakeholder on assisting or opposing the issue?

4. Which stakeholders will make what proposals to other stakeholders, strengthening or weakening coalitions?

5. Which stakeholders will revise their position on the issue resulting in anticipating the political dynamics?

3. Anticipated Dynamics

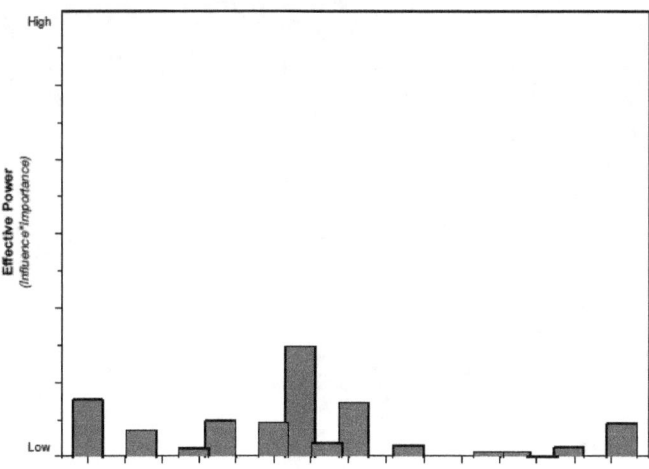

4. Modeling Iteration 2

1. How did Median position change?

2. How did risk profiles change given the change in the median position?

3. How do stakeholder perceptions change?

4. Which stakeholders will make what proposals to other stakeholders given these changes?

5. Which stakeholders will revise their position on the reform issue resulting in anticipating the political dynamics?

5. Anticipated Outcome

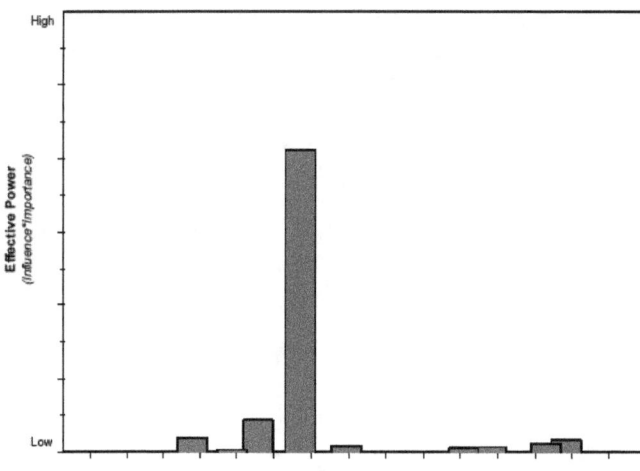

6. Interpreting Outcomes

1. Iterations stop when stakeholders see no further gains in discussions.

2. Where key stakeholders end up on the issue determines the anticipated issue outcome.

3. If a majority of stakeholders coalesce around a position, there is a large degree of consensus, if not conflict will occur.

Figure 1. Six Steps of the Senturion Modeling Process

Senturion can provide a consistent framework for objective analysis of stakeholder politics, rather than relying solely on individual expert opinions about political outcomes. Of course, analytical transformations cannot compensate for poor data. The reliance on stakeholder data—crucial to understanding human behavior and stakeholder motivations—limits the temporal forecast horizon to approximately two years, as certain data elasticities can propagate error over time. In other words, the likelihood of exogenous shocks over the stakeholder list increases over time, and after two years becomes quite high. That said, Senturion allows the analyst to examine political dynamics to, first, gauge whether the policy options are politically feasible as designed and, second, identify tactics to shape the political environment and achieve a more favorable outcome. Senturion can thus provide an assessment of multiple courses of action with a higher degree of confidence then previously available.

Having described the methodology underlying Senturion, let us turn now to a description of three recent applications.

Case Study 1: Operation Iraqi Freedom and Aftermath

This section summarizes the findings of an analysis focused on stability and regime change in Iraq. The analysis for this case study began in November 2002, while the focus of the project was on the scenario that evolved several months later, following OIF, in 2003 and 2004. Senturion was used to simulate the interactions between all stakeholders who influence Iraq's stability, forecasting the consequences for the survival of Saddam's regime and the post-Saddam period. At each stage of the analysis, the software accurately forecasted, in detail, the outcome and consequences of policy decisions regarding the U.S. military campaign in Iraq and the subsequent efforts at Iraqi reconstruction. While Senturion did a good job of anticipating the behavior of stakeholders inside Iraq, it did a poor job of anticipating the behavior of stakeholders in Europe. In general, Senturion overestimated the willingness of European stakeholders to support U.S.-led operations. While the core of the study was on Iraqi behavior, this is an important lesson learned from the case study. These inaccuracies seem to be a reflection of the level of detail applied to the data for stakeholders in Europe. For example, France and Germany were both treated as single stakeholders. In reality, the leaderships of both countries were stakeholders operating subject to domestic political constraints and concerns that affected their ability and willingness to provide support for the U.S. Thus, if the intent was to more accurately model the behavior of different coalition partners, then the stakeholder data for those potential partners should be of sufficient depth and granularity to capture the constraints they face.

All analysis was based on data provided by Iraqi subject matter experts from the Brookings Institution, RAND Corporation, and the Institute for National Strategic Studies at National Defense University. All forecasts were based on unclassified information. Updates were applied when stakeholders were captured or killed, for example, when Ali Hasan Al-Majid and Abid Hamid Hamud were captured,[10] Uday and Qusay Hussein were killed,[11] and Saddam Hussein was captured. Each new simulation, or forecast, relied on the predicted positions from the previous simulation to create a succession of simulations over a year and a half.

Based on the aftermath of OIF in April 2003, we predicted that the situation in Iraq would worsen throughout 2003 and 2004 in terms of Iraqi attitudes toward U.S. presence as well as insurgent activity. While the Senturion simulation indicated that OIF would produce a quick regime change, Saddam's well-trained former military core was expected to provide the basis for violent and persistent resistance. We anticipated that this resistance would receive broad and growing political support from numerous and otherwise opposing factions within Iraq. Initial Shiite neutrality to the United States was expected to evolve into active hostility for important factions, including al-Sadr. Ahmed Chalabi, an Iraqi dissident during the Saddam regime who was sponsored by the United States in post-war Iraq, was not expected to be a reliable ally for the United States over time. Continued U.S. military presence was expected to unify many

---

[10] Ali Hasan Al-Majid and Abid Hamid Hamud were two key leaders in Saddam's regime. Thus, we wanted to ensure that their capture would not have an appreciable change on the simulation, as they were commonly perceived as key stakeholders. Their removal did not appear to make a significant difference.

[11] Uday and Qusay Hussein, Saddam's sons, were similarly important stakeholders in his regime. Again, we wanted to update the simulation to reflect their death to ensure that the removal of such key stakeholders would not substantively impact the simulation. Their removal did not appear to make a significant difference.

Sunnis and Shiites against a common foe, the U.S. military forces on the ground. While these findings have become a more generally accepted explanation of events after the fact, there was substantial disagreement about the likely course of events as predicted by the Senturion simulation prior to OIF.

The former Iraqi regular army was expected to become an active opponent of the United States. The Kurds were expected to briefly oppose U.S. interests, but in the end renew their support for U.S. operations in Iraq. After the transfer of power on June 30, 2003, the model predicted that the French and Russians increasingly would oppose U.S. interests in Iraq. Finally, the overall level of violence in Iraq was not expected to diminish. Figure 2 shows the dates and content of the four Senturion forecasts.

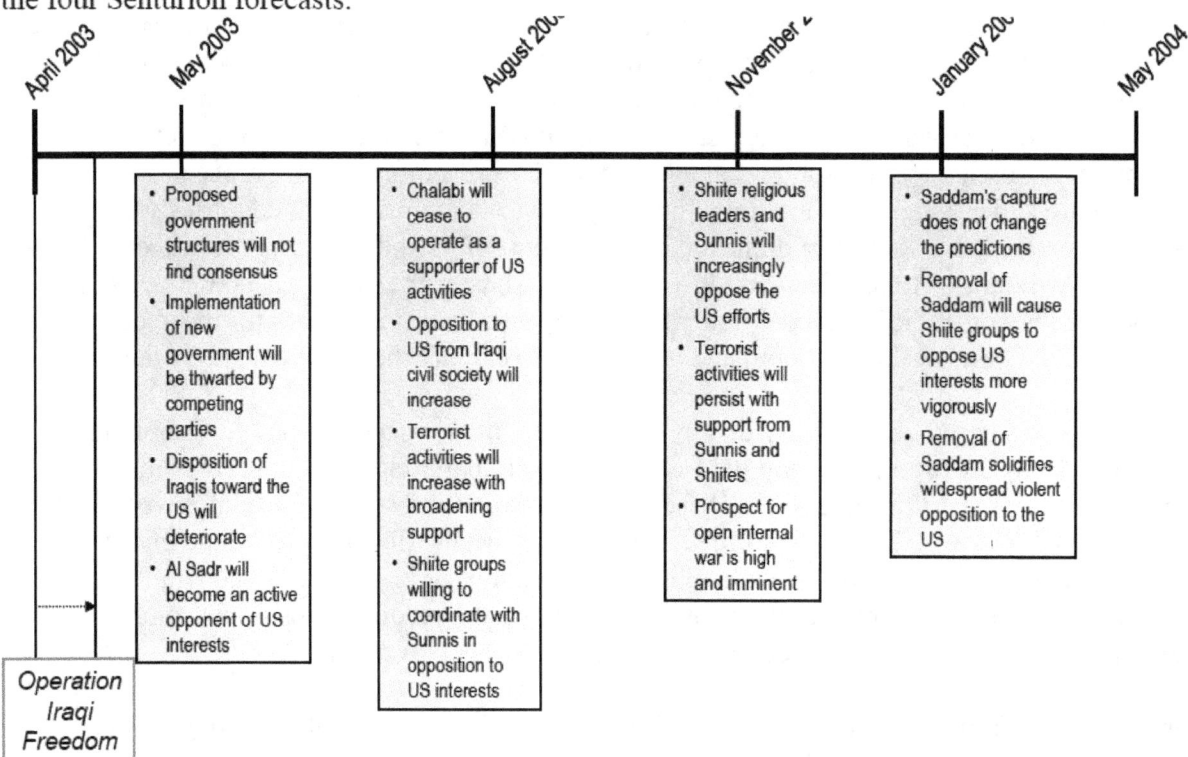

Figure 2. Track Record of Senturion Predictions on Iraq

Based on Senturion results, Saddam's inner circle was not expected to defect in the face of a U.S. military campaign or subsequent U.S. operations. The removal of Ali Hasan Al-Majid and Abid Hamid Hamud, two key leaders in Saddam's regime, as well as Saddam's sons, Qusay and Uday, was not expected to reduce the commitment of these stakeholders. Most importantly, the capture of Saddam was not expected to change these results.

The Internal Security Services, Special Security Organization, Tikriti mafia, and Special Republican Guard were well-trained and well-armed military personnel known to be extremely loyal to Saddam. From the first prediction, these groups were expected to form the core of an armed and violent resistance to U.S. operations and efforts in Iraq. Subsequent predictions and adjustments have reinforced this initial finding.

Sunni and Shiite factions were also examined to determine their likely response to the U.S. presence in Iraq. Sunni clan leaders always were expected to oppose the United States, providing support for the violent opposition to U.S. operations during and after OIF. The Sunni middle class, on the other hand, were expected to take more of a "wait and see" approach to the United States after formal military operations, and begin more vocal opposition to the U.S. activities in mid-2003. The Sunni masses were expected to remain neutral much longer, but would begin to voice mildly negative concerns in early 2004. After a brief period of support following the formal end of military operations, secular and urban Shiites were expected to oppose the United States by mid-2003. Ayatollah Ali al-Sistani and other southern Shiites were expected to remain neutral, while al-Sadr was expected to become a vocal opponent in early 2004. Most importantly, Sunni and Shiite opponents of U.S. military presence were expected to collaborate against U.S. forces. Note that this forecast was made months prior to the onset of military hostilities.

Two additional stakeholders were added to the simulation in August 2003: the Iraqi Governing Council (IGC) and Ahmed Chalabi. Chalabi was forecasted to be only a temporary ally of the United States. The IGC, on the other hand, was expected to be a consistent advocate of U.S. activities based on its close ties to the United States.

Senturion simulations provided detailed forecasts regarding how stability and regime change in Iraq would unfold as a consequence of OIF and subsequent actions. The model produced very specific predictions about the behavior of individual stakeholders and accurately captured the timing of unexpected defections as well as the potential support from unexpected allies.[12] As an experiment in applying Senturion to an unfolding political situation, our test was a success, as judged by assessments by the Defense Intelligence Agency (DIA) and Office of Secretary of Defense (OSD).[13] With only limited access to subject matter experts, robust analytic results were produced.

---

[12] For example, the specific behavior of al Sistani, al Sadr, and other Shia stakeholders following the collapse of the regime of Saddam was anticipated—to the point of even accurate sequencing of defections among different factions. Similarly, the reaction of Sunnis to the aftermath of OIF in the simulation tracked very closely to observed behavior.

[13] These assessments were documented in detail in *Predictive Analysis Pre-Select Business Case* produced by the Research and Requirements unit of the DIA on February 7, 2005.

Case Study 2: Iraqi Elections, January 2005

This section details the findings from a second analysis on Iraq, using only open-source data from subject matter experts from the Intelligence Community and Washington Institute for Near East Policy. This project focused on support for the January 2005 elections in Iraq. Once again, all findings and predictions in this briefing were generated using Senturion only. The largely pessimistic forecast for the elections held up well when compared to the actual flow of events. Table 1 summarizes all of the predictions based on data collected by the end of December 2004 and compares them to actual events that unfolded over the following two months.

Focusing on the various social factions within Iraq, Senturion provided insights into the likely behavior of Sunnis, Shia, and Kurds. The largely Sunni insurgents were expected to continue the scope and pace of attacks against supporters of the January 30, 2005 election. On the other hand, Iraqi supporters of the election, including secular Shia and Sistani's followers, would maintain their support for and participation in the election. The Sadrists were likely to lean in favor of the election over the next few weeks, but ultimately be indecisive about their support for the process. Groups neutral toward the election at the end of December 2004, including secular Sunni, the Tribal Elders, and Turkomans, were expected to remain neutral. The Kurds were in general expected to continue to support the election strongly; the PUK would be much more supportive and cooperative with Interim Prime Minister, Iyad Allawi and the interim government than the KDP.[14] Despite their mutual support for the 30 January election, tension between the Kurds and Shia was expected to remain high. Indeed, this tension is more pronounced than between Kurds and Sunnis. Finally, Senturion predicted that a change of approach that made neutral Iraqis feel safer, by either coalition forces or the insurgency, would have allowed either the U.S. or insurgents to gain the support of neutral Iraqis.

Another major question facing analysts and decisionmakers before the election was the role that other nations in the region might play. Senturion was also able to calculate both the desires and effectiveness of those stakeholders in driving the election. According to the Senturion software, Iran would attempt to drive the election, but have very little success in shaping the electoral outcome. Syrian stakeholders would have very little influence on the election. However, the U.S. (with a direct approach) was in a position to persuade the Syrian regime, Old Guard, and intelligence services to support the election with a direct request for their backing—but Syrian President Bashar al-Asad would not cooperate with such a request. Saudi Arabian and Jordanian stakeholders were expected to have very little influence on Iraqi attitudes. Finally, while Jordanian stakeholders would have little direct influence on the election, its support for the election would indirectly solidify the support of Shia tribal elements.

---

[14] The two leading Kurdish groups in Iraq are the Patriotic Union of Kurdistan (PUK), led by Jalal Talabani, and the Kurdish Democratic Party (KDP), led by Massoud Barzani.

Predictions *(Based on 12/30/2004 Data)*	Actual Events	Date of Actual Event
Insurgents will continue scope and pace of attacks.	Repeated attacks by insurgents continued through the elections.	1/31/2005[15]
Strong supporters of the elections, particularly Sistani's followers and secular Shia, will participate in the election.	Sistani's supporters and secular Shia voted in large numbers in the election.	2/1/2005[16]
Sadrists will be indecisive about supporting the election despite positive signs during January.	Sadrists straddle both sides of the election issue, neither boycotting nor actively opposing the election, but also not endorsing the process.	1/31/2005[17]
Secular Sunnis and Sunni tribal elders will remain neutral toward the election.	Sunnis disproportionately stayed home during the election, while not actively opposing the process.	2/1/2005[18]
Kurds will strongly support the election.	Kurds turned out for the election in large numbers.	2/1/2005[19]
Tension will remain high between Kurds and Shia.	Tension between Kurds and Shia on future of Iraq appears to remain high despite the election.	1/31/2005[20]
Zarqawi and foreign insurgents will have little success in undermining support for election in January.	Election went forward with high Shia participation, despite attacks by insurgents.	2/1/2005[21]
World Bank and IMF will pull back support of the election.	Timing and willingness of World Bank and IMF reconstruction efforts in Iraq unclear.	1/28/2005[22]
France, Russia, and Germany will increasingly support the election.	France and Germany praise the Iraqi election. Russian response ambiguous.	2/2/2005[23]

Table 1. Track Record of Iraqi Election Predictions

---

[15] *Washington Times*, Jan 31, 2005.

[16] *Washington Post*, Feb 1, 2005.

[17] *New York Times*, Jan 31, 2005.

[18] *Washington Times*, Feb 1, 2005.

[19] *Washington Times*, Feb 1, 2005.

[20] *Christian Science Monitor*, Jan 31, 2005.

[21] *Washington Post*, Feb 1, 2005.

[22] *Washington Post*, Jan 28, 2005.

[23] *International Herald Tribune*, Feb 2, 2005.

Senturion also was used to assess the reactions to the election of major players in the international community. France, Russia, and Germany were expected to coalesce and increasingly support the election, but their impact would be minimal on Iraqi attitudes. Poland, South Korea, and Australia would continue to strongly support the election with limited impact on Iraqi attitudes. Turkey, Ukraine, Egypt, and Japan would also remain supportive of the election. Finally, the World Bank and IMF were expected to quickly pull back their explicit support for the election.

In assessing the insurgency in Iraq, Senturion provided two startling conclusions. As for foreign insurgents, Senturion forecasted that Zarqawi and other foreign insurgents had very little leverage to undermine support for the election at this point. On the other hand, domestic insurgents, composed mainly of former regime elements, had most of the leverage in this situation in the months before the election. However, they did not recognize the extent of their potential influence. As long as the highly-trained factions of the former regime elements focused indiscriminately on targets in Iraq, they missed out on an opportunity to capture the support of neutral Iraqis. Were the former regime elements to shift their tactics and focus solely on coalition forces and their closest allies, they would maximize their leverage and better achieve their goal of minimizing support for the election. Such a shift by the insurgents would have undermined the resolve of the coalition to push forward on the elections and solidified the support of neutral Iraqis for the insurgency by making them feel safer. We cannot assess the accuracy of this finding because the former regime elements did not exploit this opportunity.

Senturion also can be used to test alternative courses of action. The assumptions, policies, and tactics of U.S. stakeholders can be simulated to identify first- and second-order consequences, then adjusted to find the optimal approach to a particular situation. Moreover, because Senturion calculates the perceptions of stakeholders, it can also identify circumstances when perceptions of key stakeholders are inaccurate. At times, such knowledge may form the basis for a course of action to exploit the limits of perception. Several courses of action to improve the situation in Iraq prior to the election were identified using Senturion, as described below.

First, Senturion identified a way to persuade Sunni tribal elements to moderate their opposition to the election. Initially, Interim Prime Minister Allawi and the interim government would have needed to alter their approach to the Sunni tribes and focus on persuading the youth element in the Sunni tribes. The youths could have been offered a modest monetary incentive to take a neutral stance toward the elections. After this accomplishment, the Sunni tribal elders could have been approached to actively support the elections (as the tribes would not have been split if the elders had accepted such an offer at that point). In a truly tribal structure, the elders decide on the course of the tribe and the youth will follow. However, no individuals make decisions without observing the sentiment and preferences of those around them. In this case, the model indicated that the elders were weakly committed to their initial course of action and could have been persuaded by the opinions of tribal youths, which in turn could have been influenced by U.S. strategic messaging or an information operation campaign.

Second, we identified a way to obtain support from some former regime elements. Specifically, Senturion analysis suggested that rank and file former regime elements could have been persuaded to participate in the election if directly approached by Interim Prime Minister Allawi with U.S. backing. More senior and better trained former regime elements were not expected to respond to such an approach. These two measures would not have lessened the insurgency, but according to the Senturion simulation, they could have increased Sunni participation in the election.

Finally, Senturion was used to assess the implication of adjusting the force structure in Iraq before the election. A reduced coalition military presence in Iraq would not have appreciably affected the attitudes of Iraqi stakeholders. However, increased coalition military strength in Iraq would have improved the attitudes of Iraqi stakeholders toward the election by making them feel more secure. We tested a variety of different options for the composition of military forces, as well as the level of percentage increase in forces on the ground necessary to impose the peace. The scenarios tested included the following, with the associated impact of each increase in boots on the ground:

- 25% increase in coalition military strength would have captured the support of neutral Iraqis.
- 50% increase in coalition military strength would have captured the support of neutral and some opposing Iraqis.
- 75-100% increase in coalition military strength would have captured the support of neutral Iraqis, but with less gain in support than with a 50% increase.

After testing the impact of greater numbers of troops, we also tested whether the population would be sensitive to the composition of enhanced deployments, that is, would it make a different if the troops were composed of strictly U.S. forces or a combination with other allied forces. The Senturion analysis indicated that the composition of U.S. versus other coalition troops did not make a difference in perceptions of the Iraqi population. However, there was a difference when testing the perception of using United Nations peacekeepers in place of U.S. troops, in that they could play a similar peacekeeping and policing role to that of U.S. or coalition military forces, but because of the perceptions of Iraqis, could accomplish the same results with fewer troops.

The final set of Senturion simulations focused on scenarios that might have disrupted progress toward elections. In particular, we found that the assassination of al Sistani, al Sadr, or Allawi would not have disrupted support for or opposition to the election. The finding on al Sistani was a dramatic change from earlier findings on his role in Iraq. Over the course of the analyses in 2003 and 2004 as described above, al Sistani played a major stabilizing role, and his death would have caused even greater instability. However, during the final run-up to the election, he had clearly declared his support for the U.S.-led elections. By no longer occupying a neutral role, the important stabilizing role previously played by al Sistani was diminished. Similarly, removal of Zarqawi was unlikely to disrupt the insurgents or affect support for the election. Finally, a targeted reduction of former regime element capability would have had little or no impact on support for the election.

Case Study 3: Palestinian Leadership Transition after Yasser Arafat's Death

These results are drawn from a study analysis for the DIA on the leadership transition in Palestine following the death of Arafat and its impact on the Palestinian-Israeli peace negotiations. Unclassified data were collected from subject matter experts in the Intelligence Community on November 2, 2004, immediately following Arafat's death and prior to the consolidation of power in Palestine. Table 2 summarizes the track record of these predictions.

Predictions (Based on 11/2/2004 Data)	Actual Events	Date of Actual Event
Fatah old guard will quickly support Mazen.	15-member Central Committee endorses Mazen.	11/23/2004[24]
Mazen will quickly persuade Qaddumi and Dahlan to lend their support.	Both Qaddumi and Dahlan endorse Mazen as President of the Palestinian Authority.	11/22/2004[25]
Mazen expected to work with Dahlan and Musa Arafat, arranging power sharing accommodations with each.	Dahlan and Musa Arafat reconcile their violent differences under the guidance of Mazen and lend their support.	11/21/2004[26]
Israel and Europe expected to accept Mazen's leadership role.	Mazen is the favored choice of Israel and Europe for Palestinian leadership.	11/24/2004[27]
After most have declared support for Mazen, the AAMB will lend its support.	AAMB factions issued a joint statement calling for Palestinians to support Mazen.	11/28/2004[28]
Barghouti not expected to oppose Mazen—risk of opposition alliance with Hamas or AAMB.	Barghouti endorses Mazen.	11/26/2004[29]
	Barghouti enters presidential race.	12/1/2004[30]
	Barghouti withdraws from presidential race.	12/12/2004[31]

Table 2. Track Record of Palestinian Leadership Transition Predictions

---

[24] *Washington Post*, Nov 23, 2004.
[25] Arabic Media Network, Nov 22, 2004.
[26] *Jerusalem Post*, Nov 21, 2004.
[27] *The Guardian*, Nov 24, 2004.
[28] BBC News, Nov 28, 2004.
[29] United Press International, Nov 26, 2004.
[30] *Jerusalem Post*, Dec 2, 2004.
[31] BBC News, Dec 12, 2004.

Senturion accurately anticipated that Abu Mazen (a name applied to Mahmoud Abbas as a sign of respect) would be accepted as a political leader by the Presidential election in January 2005. Despite initial wide variance in the level of support from Palestinian stakeholders, as well as initial opposition by several militant groups within Palestine, all opposition to his leadership role was expected to erode.

Senturion predicted a consolidation of Palestinian support for Mazen through leadership power-sharing arrangements. Of those supporting Mazen, most were expected to support his leadership around the position of Abu Ala (also known as Ahmed Ali Mohammed Qurei, a member of the Fatah Central Committee). Mazen was expected to soften his claims to leadership first in response to Mohammed Dahlan (member of the Palestinian Legislative Council), and then in response to Musa Arafat (nephew of Yasser Arafat), implying some sort of power-sharing accommodation with each.

Protracted opposition by armed groups was not expected. Mazen was expected to quickly persuade the Fatah hardliners, Faruq al-Qaddumi (interim chairman of the Fatah[32]), and Musa Arafat to support him. A year later, in September 2005, Musa Arafat was murdered, but during the course of the Palestinian election, Senturion correctly anticipated relative calm among these political figures. Hamas and the Al Aqsa Martyrs' Brigades (AAMB)[33] were anticipated to respond to this consolidation by softening their level of opposition. Over time, the Senturion analysis indicated that both the AAMB and Hamas would realize they must support Mazen or risk being isolated from all other stakeholders.

The major risk to this consolidation of power was the formation of an alliance between Marwan Barghouti (a leader of the Fatah movement imprisoned in Israel) and more extreme opponents of Mazen. In the early stages of Mazen's consolidation of support, immediately after Arafat's death, Senturion found that either AAMB or Hamas had the potential to bring Barghouti into an opposition coalition. Such a coalition would have posed the risk of a violent transition, as some of its members had previously relied on violence to express their opposition. However, this coalition was considered unlikely to form, as the AAMB and others were not expected to consider it workable.

Figures 3 and 4 show the distribution of effective power (influence weighted by importance) in support of particular positions, so that the strength of various coalitions can be easily identified. Figure 3 shows the distribution of power as of 2 November, 2004, and indicates a wide variety of positions supported by stakeholders. This indicated very little consensus regarding the choice of Mazen as the next Palestinian leader.

---

[32] At the time of this study, and even today to a lesser extent, Fatah was the major political party in Palestine. Fatah is the reverse acronym from the Arabic name Harakat al-Tahrir al-Watani al-Filastini (literally: "Palestinian National Liberation Movement"), and it is the largest organization within the Palestine Liberation Organization (PLO), a multi-party confederation. Thus, it was important for Abu Mazen to obtain the support of Fatah.

[33] The Al Aqsa Martyrs' Brigades are a Palestinian armed terrorist group closely linked to the Fatah party. It is often considered the radical militant arm of Fatah, although the ties between the organizations are not entirely clear. This militia was originally named after the Al Aqsa Mosque, one of Islam's holiest sites and an icon for the Palestinian movement.

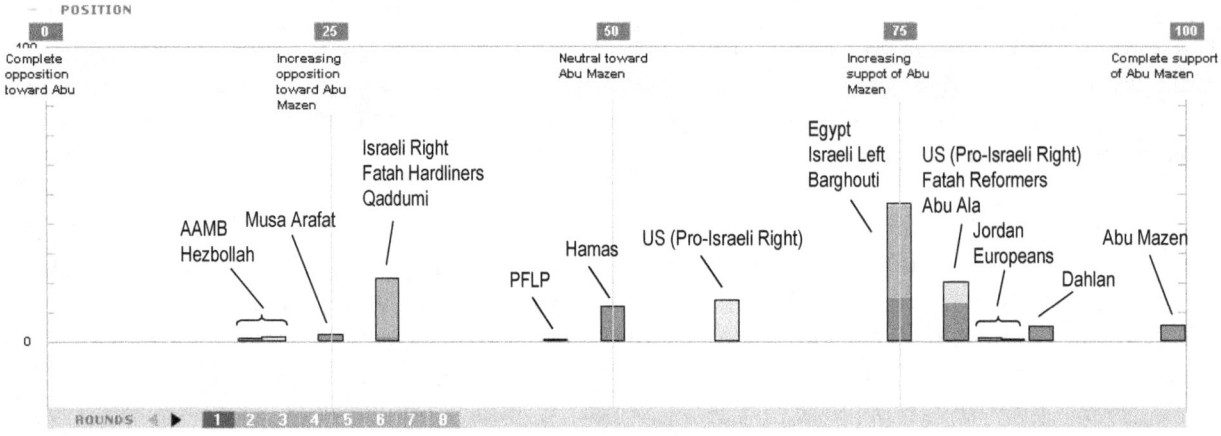

Figure 3. Current Situation - Distribution of Stakeholder Advocated Positions in Support of or in Opposition to Abu Mazen

Figure 4, on the other, hand, reflects the distribution of effective power after the passage of several political interactions. This figure indicates that, over time, Mazen will consolidate support of all stakeholders. However, since all stakeholders have coalesced around a position less extreme than complete support of Mazen as Palestinian leader, we infer that he will accommodate others within the leadership and has agreed to some sort of power-sharing arrangement—while still taking the lead role in his coalition.

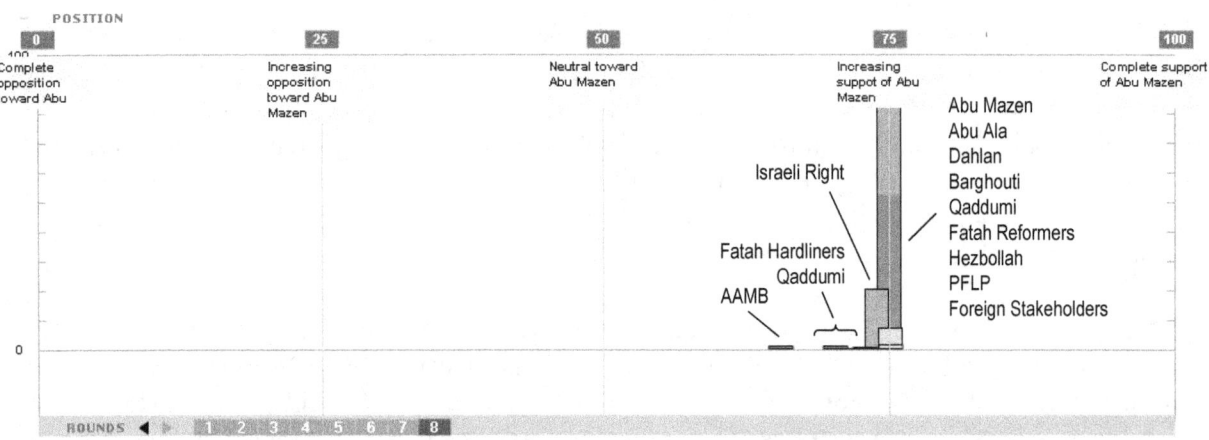

Figure 4. Predicted Situation (Round 8 of simulation, approximately 10-14 weeks) Distribution of Stakeholder Advocated Positions in Support of or in Opposition to Abu Mazen

Figures 5 and 6 provide a round-by-round view of the position shifts of stakeholders, based on the Senturion calculations. According to a tracking of actual events, as documented in Table 2, these predictions proved to be uniformly accurate. While the software takes into consideration the influence of all stakeholders to more clearly identify changes in stakeholder positions over time, figure 5 depicts only Palestinian positions and figure 6 depicts only the positions of foreign stakeholders.

Figure 5 indicated that, of those supporting Mazen, most would consolidate their position around Abu Ala, Barghouti, and the Fatah Reformers. Mazen is persuaded to soften his claims to leadership first in response to Dahlan, and then in response to Musa Arafat, suggesting some sort of accommodation with each.

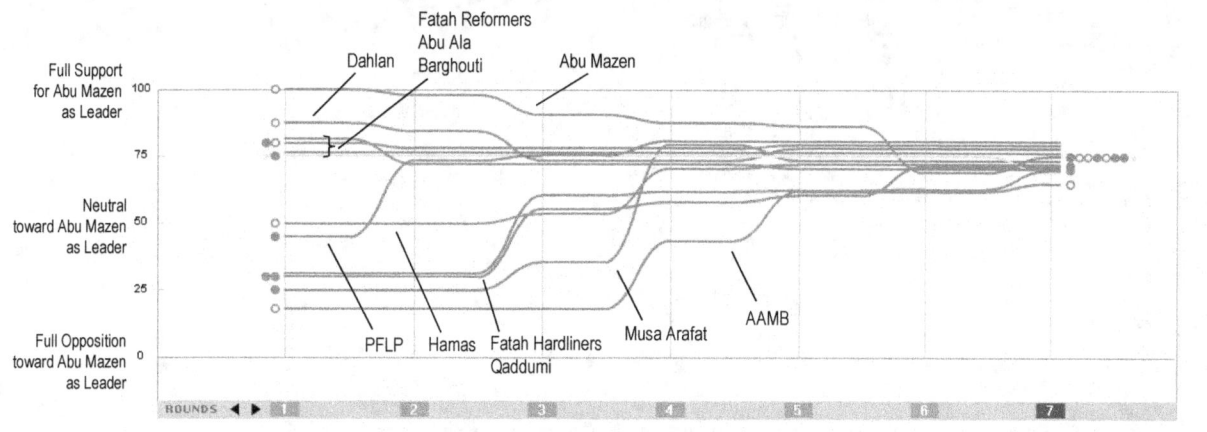

Figure 5. Prediction of 8 Rounds of Stakeholder Position Shifts
Position Shifts of Palestinian Stakeholders' Support of or Opposition to Abu Mazen

At the other end of the spectrum, stakeholders opposed to Mazen were persuaded to lend their support to his leadership. Mazen was able to persuade the Fatah Hardliners, Qaddumi, and Musa Arafat to support him in the second round of the simulation. Hamas and the AAMB responded to this consolidation by increasing their level of support for him. In the third round, Hamas was persuaded by the new Palestinian leadership coalition to back Mazen. The AAMB, initially the most ardent opponent of Mazen, then had to make concessions or risk being isolated from all other stakeholders. Thus, even the AAMB was persuaded by Mazen and then Musa Arafat to support the coalition.

Figure 6 provides a summary of expected position shifts for international stakeholders. Barghouti's support for Mazen appeared to be important for validating the Mazen coalition in the eyes of foreign opponents, including such disparate stakeholders as the Israeli Right, Hezbollah, Iran, and Syria. As with the Palestinian stakeholders, all stakeholders came to support the Mazen coalition after several rounds of the simulation exercise.

AAMB, according to Senturion, was a critical stakeholder in the evolution of support for Mazen. In the early stages of Mazen's consolidation of support, the AAMB and other opponents had the potential to bring Barghouti into a prospective opposition coalition. Such a coalition would have raised the risk of a violent transition, as some of its members had previously expressed their opposition through violence.

However, Senturion indicated that AAMB was unlikely to realize the potential success of such an initiative. If they, or other more extreme opponents of Mazen, realized the viability of such a coalition, the result was likely to be entrenched and potentially violent opposition to his leadership coalition—preventing the consolidation of support from any of his more extreme opponents.

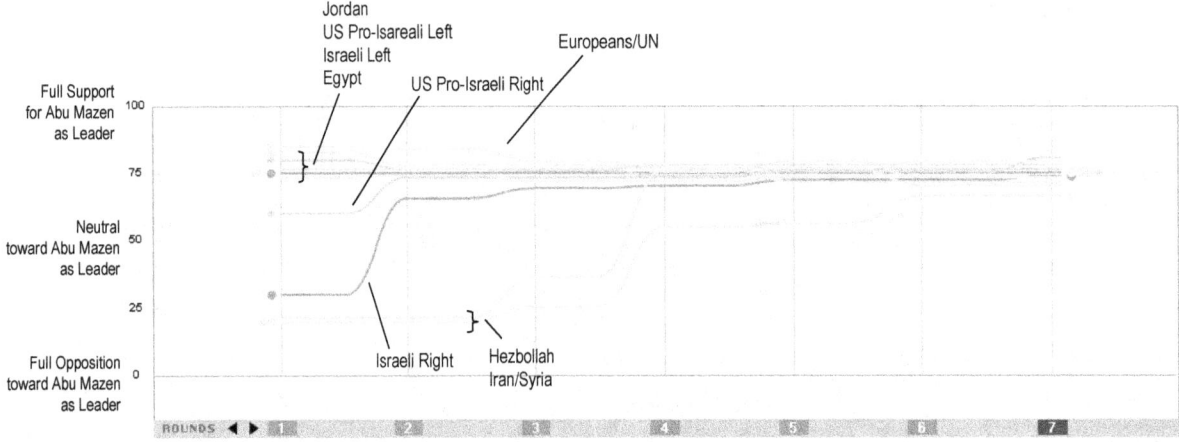

Figure 6. Prediction of 8 Rounds of Stakeholder Position Shifts
Position Shifts of International Stakeholders' Support of or Opposition to Abu Mazen

Conclusions

The three case studies described above demonstrate a portion of the track record of predictions that were produced by the Senturion software. This approach could compliment traditional analysis by allowing for the exploration of multiple permutations and iterations of analyst assumptions within a consistent framework. Moreover, systematic and rigorous tools such as Senturion enable analysts to generate courses of action to obtain improved outcomes and mitigate the risk associated with uncertain approaches.

A predictive political simulation technology such as Senturion can be applied to an array of political-military problems in near-real-time. Approaches such as Senturion are useful in the complex field of predictive analysis because they facilitate a systematic account of stakeholder interactions, with a reliable predictive tool to support the decisionmaking and analytic processes. As shown in these case studies (and in all document DOD and Intelligence Community studies), Senturion has been uncannily accurate at anticipating stakeholder behavior. However, the greater aid that the tool offers is in providing analysts and decisionmakers with an alternative and systematic view of the decisionmaking process. By keeping track of and simulating stakeholder behavior in a systematic fashion, Senturion is able to identify subtle dynamics between stakeholders that might not otherwise be apparent. The combination of these subtle behaviors produces a rich, detailed view of stakeholder dynamics that in turn provides a capability that can be used to help test hypotheses and often produce counter intuitive results. Combined with subject matter expert input, Senturion provides a visualization and forecast of evolving political environments that can be adjusted in real time to see varying results and implications for differing courses of action. While analytical tools will never replace the human analyst, Senturion can help leverage analysts' time to produce more accurate and actionable assessments of complex political-military situations.

Bibliography

Abdollahian, Mark and Carole Alsharabati. 2003. "Modeling the Strategic Effects of Risk and Perceptions in Linkage Politics." *Rationality and Society*. Winter. Available at: http://rss.sagepub.com/.

Axelrod, Robert and Leigh Tesfatsion. 2005. "A Guide For Newcomers To Agent-Based Modeling In The Social Sciences." Forthcoming in the *Handbook of Computational Economics*, Vol. 2: Agent-Based Computational Economics, Kenneth L. Judd and Leigh Tesfatsion (eds.), North-Holland. Available at: http://www.econ.iastate.edu/tesfatsi/hbace.htm.

Axtell, Robert, Robert Axelrod, Joshua M. Epstein, and Michael D. Cohen. 1996. "Aligning Simulation Models: A Case Study and Results." *Computational and Mathematical Organization Theory*. 1(2):123-141.

Bueno de Mesquita, Bruce. 1981. The *War Trap.* New Haven, Yale University Press.

Caldwell, Steven B. 1997. "Dynamic Microsimulation and the Corsim 3.0 Model." Ithaca, NY: Strategic Forecasting.

Chwe, Michael Suk-Young. 1999. "Structure and Strategy in Collective Action." *American Journal of Sociology*. 105(1): 128-56.

Coplin, William D., and Michael K. O'Leary. 1972. *Everyman's Prince: A Guide to Understanding Your Political Problems*. North Scituate, MA: Duxbury Press.

Epstein, J and R. Axtell. 1996. *Growing Artificial Societies: Social Science from the Bottom Up*. Cambridge, MA: MIT Press.

Feder, Stanley. Declassified 1994. "Factions and Policon: New Ways to Analyze Politics." *Studies in Intelligence*, Central Intelligence Agency.

Halal, William E., and Gary Bojes. 2005. "Evaluation of Forecasting Methods." *Futures Research Quarterly*. Vol. 21, No. 1.

Kugler, Jacek, and Yi Feng, eds. 1997. "The Expected Utility Approach to Policy Decision Making." *International Interactions*. Vol. 23, No. 3-4.

Lalman, David. 1988. "Conflict Resolution and Peace." *American Journal of Political Science*. Vol. 32, No. 3.

Macy, Michael W. and Robert Willer. 2001. "From Factors to Actors: Computational Sociology and Agent-Based Modeling." Cornell University manuscript.

Marrin, Stephen. 2002. "Homeland Security and the Analysis of Foreign Intelligence." Markle Foundation Task Force on National Security in the Information Age.

Morgan, T. Clifton, 1994. *Untying the Knot of War*. Ann Arbor, MI: University of Michigan Press.

Morrow, James D. 1986. "A Spatial Model of International Conflict." *American Political Science Review*. Vol. 80, No. 4.

Rieber, Steven. 2004. "Intelligence Analysis and Judgmental Calibration." *International Journal of Intelligence and Counterintelligence.*